BLACK BUTTERFLY

OTHER BOOKS BY ROBERT M. DRAKE

SPACESHIP (2012)

SCIENCE (2013)

BEAUTIFUL CHAOS (2014)

A BRILLIANT MADNESS (2015)

BEAUTIFUL AND DAMNED (2016)

BLACK
BUTTERFLY

ROBERT M. DRAKE

Andrews McMeel
Publishing®

a division of Andrews McMeel Universal

Andrews McMeel Publishing
a division of Andrews McMeel Universal
1130 Walnut Street, Kansas City, Missouri 64106

www.andrewsmcmeel.com

16 17 18 19 20 RR2 10 9 8 7 6 5 4 3 2 1

ISBN: 978-1-4494-8479-8

Library of Congress Control Number: 2016946061

Book design: Robert M. Drake

First Edition 2015

Dedicated

to all who have a dream

to all who struggle
two jobs to get by

to all who have been
ignored all their lives

to all who feel empty

to all who cannot sleep
because there is so much
in their mind

to all who have died a little
in the name of love

to all who are called weird,
strange and odd

to all who create because
that is the only thing they know
how to do

to all who believe in something

to all who breathe and to all
who are no longer here

this one is for you.

The world is filled
with broken people
with broken lives
searching for broken love.
And that is why being
alone has never
felt so good.

I can't see myself
with the crowd.

I never have.

We are the manifestation
of a wild dream.

CONTENTS

BLACK BUTTERFLY

Love is a violent
flower blooming in
the middle of my bones.

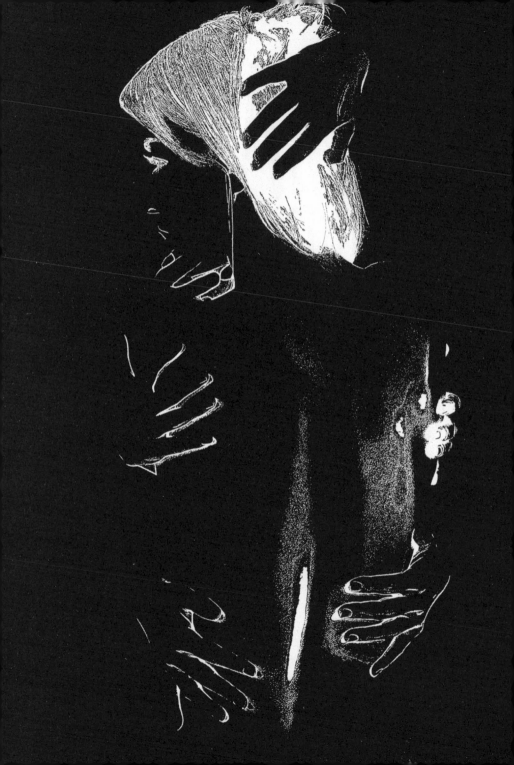

Inner Truth

The funny thing
about
advice is,
we always tell
others
the things
we
cannot
really do
ourselves.

No One Will

I know how you feel
when you're alone,
lying on your bed,
looking at your phone
as if it's meant
to bring you peace from
all the demons tugging
at your head.

You ask yourself:
"who in the world will love me?"
and you should always
remember how no one will
not ever,
unless you love
yourself.

The Spaces We Leave

I can't recognize myself
lately;
I'm someone I used to know.
I think you took me with you
and I was hoping you could
just leave me somewhere else,
because I've been waiting
for myself,
waiting for all the pieces
to come home.

Deserve To Expect

Maybe all that we are
is what
people expect us
to be.

Or maybe we are more
and we expect
much less
than we think we deserve.

Save You

Open those
eyes
there is so
much
around you,
and give this
world
a
chance to
save you.

Love & Stars

Love
what loves you,
but never
hate
what hates you.
For hate is
the burden
to exhaust
the
stars in you.

Old Photographs

We take pictures with people
so they could remember us
and leave memories behind
so they don't forget us.
And the difference
between the two is the same.

We leave these moments
in the air,
hoping that somewhere
someone will find them
and make sense of everything
we chose to ignore.

Messages To You

My Dear,
Sometimes I am here
and sometimes I am not,
I like that about myself
for I am folded.
But please guide me
in the right direction,
for sometimes I, too,
tend to lose myself
in my imagination.

Believe

I need to believe
that only I can chase
my dreams.
That only I can light the
fire in me.
That no one can break me
unless I break myself and
only someone else can help
me carry my pieces. I need
to believe that I am
different and I am full of
love. And if I live every
moment believing, then the
chaos in my heart will
be a beautiful thing, and
the world will never cease
to forget my name.

I just need to believe.

Be Better

How are we
supposed to love
one another
when we barely love
ourselves.

We are so much
better than
what they want
us to be.

Heaven & Hell

I found heaven and hell
in people
and those places could never
be ignored.
Because there are more truths
buried deep within us
than any science or religion
would ever allow to be revealed.

These are the hidden secrets.

We are all our own
form of destruction,
and our existence
is an act of our
own choices.

Forgetting How

Too often
we feel
like we don't know
how to live,
and too often
someone will tell you how;
without them
even knowing
how to live
for themselves.

Confused Letters

Because
sometimes,
the people we
need to save us,
are really
the people who
need the saving
for themselves.

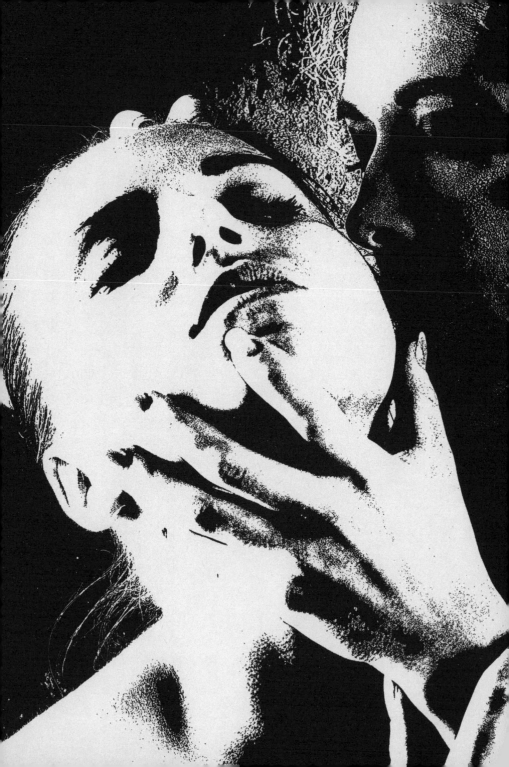

She Loves

Then,
she began to breathe,
and live,
and every moment took her
to a place
where good-byes were hard
to come by.
She was in love,
but not in love with
someone or something;
she was in love with her
life.

And for the first time,
in a long time,
everything
was inspiring.

What I Meant To Say

People are all the same
but you and I,
we're not like them.
So to say that we'll both stay
isn't you and it isn't me
either.
We're tragically drawn
to one another
and eventually we'll fall apart.
So let's enjoy
whatever it is that we have,
because when we're done,
I wouldn't know what else
to give you
other than just another story.
And that alone might be
the most beautiful thing
we'll ever live to tell.

Scars & Dreams

Sometimes,
your scars have a lot
less to do
with where you have been
and a lot more
to do
with where you are going.

Hello Again

And in the end,
letting go was
a lot like finding
love.
I had to learn
to say good-bye
to the one
who gave me the
courage to say
hello.

Fear

Destroy the
fear in you
before the
fear destroys
the life
before you.

Relatable Chaos

From chaos to lullabies
I watched her
live my thoughts,
and soon enough
she did become
my favorite story.
She was everything
and with every word
she drew me closer.
She drew me into her story,
a story
I knew I would never
be able to understand.

And I...

And I loved her,
all of her,
for how I watched her
crawl beneath my skin
and into my soul.

And I loved her,
all of her,
for how she would glide
over my dark fields
and leave trails of roses
left to grow.

And I loved her,
all of her,
for how she devoured
me whole
and made sense
of all of my bones.

But most of all,
I loved her,
all of her,
for healing my pieces
and guiding them
all back home.

Finding Nothing

And for once
I did not know
where to
begin,
I felt like
I have been looking,
looking for a
love that I
have already
lost.

Beautiful Chaos

Chaos,
leave me never,
keep me wild
and keep me free
so that my
brokenness will be,
the only beauty
the world will see.

Let Live

I was born
the moment
I fell in love
with the world,
because I knew,
somewhere,
someone like you
existed in it.

Unheard Glory

If there is something
you must know
before I let you go;
it is this:
in your journey
you will meet
broken people,
hateful people,
and people
who have lost the sight
for their glory.

And the beauty
of it all is this:
I will tell you
to love them,
to love them deeply
and show them
how some of us
still care.

Never give up on them,
for to give up on them
is to destroy
a reflection
of ourselves.

I Did Not Know

I couldn't find the
words to save you,
to make you still.

And I buried myself
in the regret
until I became it.

If only I had
known,
then perhaps,
you
would have stayed.

Small Heroes

How beautifully blind
are we
to ignore the
smallest things
in us,
for it is the smallest parts
in us
that give us
the power to do
the most brilliant
of things.

Feel The Moment

When it was over,
nothing defined us,
other than
the moments
that made us feel
free.

We Must Be Mad

It must be madness
the way we let
things devour us,
the way we let
the things we want out
back in.

And the horror of it all
is this:
we stay attracted
to everything that hurts.
We cling to it
and never really learn
to let go.

So perhaps,
we do want happiness,
but we also desire to keep
the pain close.
Close enough to destroy us,
close enough to define us,
and close enough
to make us feel
a little less cold.

No Air Here

I cannot say
that I do not
want to drown.
I just hope it is
you
that will be there
when I let go
because you are
the reason
I lose my breath
every time I try
to breathe.

Lost World

Maybe that is
the problem
with the world.
We do not know
what to feel
and
we do not know
how to be
ourselves.

Thinking Kills

We think
we owe everyone
something.
We think
we need to
explain ourselves
and we think
too much
about
thinking too much.

And it is funny
how we think
we know it all,
but the reality is
this:
everything we think
that brings us closer
together
is everything
that sets us
further apart.
And overthinking how
different we all are
is failing
to recognize how connected
we all could really be.

I Wanted To Talk

It took me years
to understand
that the more
I tried to settle her flames,
the bigger her fire grew.
And the more I tried
to control her
the further I pushed her
away.

And when she was finally
gone,
she left nothing behind.
And for some reason
I still thought of her;
I still hoped
that maybe somewhere,
someone has found her
and has finally
learned
how to set her heart
free.

Heal

To change the world
we must
heal our women,
because it is the
women who teach us
how to love.
And if a man can learn
to love,
the way a woman
loves a child
then that man will
see the world
in a different light.

The world
will never be
the same.

Remember Me

I hope there is
someone
to remember me,
when the world
has forgotten.

I hope there is
someone
to love me,
when love
has forgotten.

I hope it is
you who finds me,
when I have lost
hope
in everything
I used to
live for.

Make Me Stay

All the people
we have met
and all the people
we have yet to meet
are meant to exist
so we can find them.
So we both
could exchange
a set of directions,
directions which will
guide us to the next
place
we are meant to go.

And as we go;
we must always believe
that maybe this
could be our last stop.
That maybe the next
person we meet
will not have a set of
directions,
that maybe they will have
more,
and that maybe they will offer us
something beautiful enough
to inspire us to stay.

Fatally Yours

Our fate lies
in the hands
of the things we love
and sometimes
the things we love
are the things
that lead us
to the fatal destruction
of ourselves.

Time Changes

The hardest part
is
accepting how
people change
and
that alone
changes everything.

Life & Death

How beautiful it is
to live in a world
where nothing lasts
forever.
We must learn to
fall in love with
the love inside
us.

Only then,
every moment living
will be
every moment
worth dying for.

Closer

Because sometimes
it never makes any sense;
the more I try to forget,
the more everything
reminds me.
The more I try
to run away,
the closer I am
to it all.
The more I try
to be different,
the more I realize
that I am the same.

Because sometimes
nothing ever makes any sense,
but also because
sometimes
what doesn't make any sense
is everything I need
to define all that I
feel.

Rain Fall

And
all I could
remember
was the two of us
lying on the ground
and looking
at the sky,
wishing for it to rain.
In hopes
that maybe
we both
could learn a little something
about falling
the way the sky
wrote it
on the clouds.

Dead Thrills

It takes a certain
kind of courage to love.
It is not easy and I
always know how these
things end,
sometimes dull and
sometimes boring.

People are easy to lose
the thrill of being
with the same person,
especially for a long
time.

We are like that and
nothing ever survives time.
Give anything a little
time, and soon enough
that clock
will end.

No Ears

Sometimes,
we hate ourselves
for the
feelings we
ignore.

Maybe that is
the problem;
we do not listen
to ourselves
until it is
too late.

I Am The Fire

Listen,
I am not someone
who is easy to love.
I am not someone
who is to be taken
lightly
and most of all
I am not someone
to burn.

For I am the fire,
my soul is on fire
and everything I live to
touch
becomes one with
the fire.

So ask yourself
if you are willing
to burn,
because the moment
you open yourself to me,
I will have no choice
but to scorch everything
that defines you.
And without regret
I will devour
and I will leave nothing
behind.

Home Is People

There will be times
when we feel like we are meant
to be alone;
like this love we seek is not
real and we created it
to make sense of our
emptiness.

And because of that,
sometimes, some of us become
bitter with the idea
that love is only the
anticipation of finding someone
we will never live to meet.

So we live our lives looking
for something to fill us
and give us meaning,
only to discover
that in the end,
love was never meant to be
received by one person,
but rather all the people
who made us feel at home.

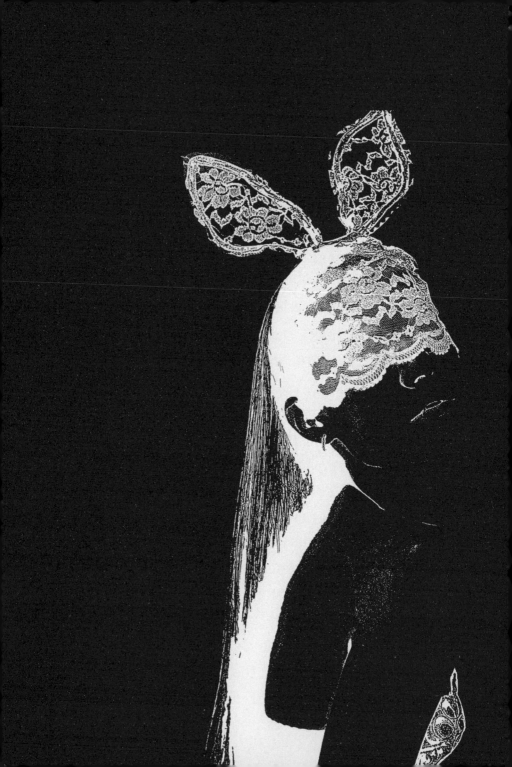

Save Everyone

And every night
she would change herself,
stay up late
and grow deeper
in love.
She wanted to love
it all,
everything and everyone.

And how ironic was it,
she wanted to save
the world,
the same world
who could not
remember her name.

Close Strangers

And in that moment,
all I could
remember was our
good-bye
and how every moment
spent
was like I never
knew you at all.

Minds

We are all
born to suffer
from truths
and we are all
born to live
from lies.

And sometimes
the darkness
feels closer to
heaven
than any light
that might direct
us closer to
hell.

Love Moments

Tragedies will always
be found in the things
we love
and if we are not willing
to see
the beauty in losing something
that means the world
to us,
then imagine how terrible
it will be to live for them.

We must always
welcome the end
of all things.
For sometimes knowing nothing
lasts forever,
is the only way we can learn
to fall in love
with all the moments,
and all the people,
that are meant to take
our breath away.

The Worlds In Us

The world tells us
we are different,
and I laugh.
I laugh because
we are all products
of its misery.

We are all
alone and lost,
the same way
the world stays in the
heart of it all.

Alone and lost
between the darkness.

Alone and lost
we are the same.

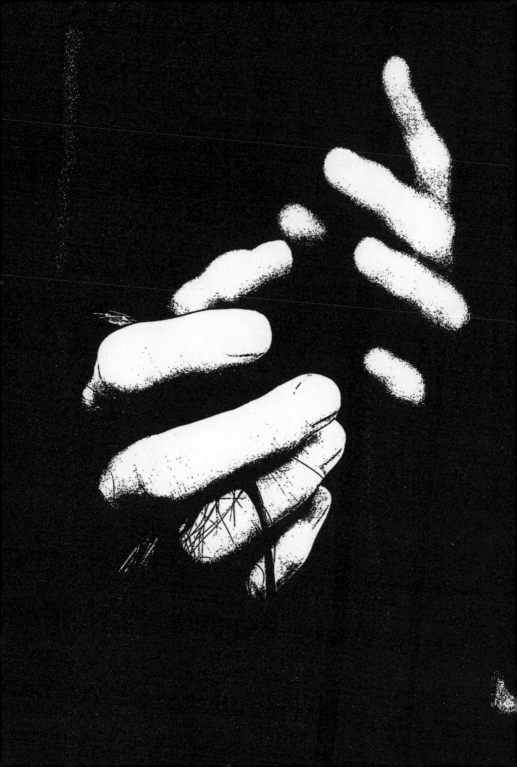

I Love Her

And she
always had a way
with her
brokenness.

She would
take her pieces
and make them
beautiful.

Expressions

I could never see
the world in the same light,
because love has made me
believe
that sometimes the soul
could feel the things
that the body would never
be able to understand.

And that within itself
would be the perfect expression.
Where all the things
I shared with the world
were never meant to be understood,
but rather
to be poured deeply
within their hearts
and
be felt.

Endless War

After all, war is all that
we are and everything we do is
fought like one.
We fight to survive,
we fight for people we love,
and we fight against ourselves.

And these wars are the only
things that make sense to us.
It is all we have ever known
and that alone has everything
to do with everything we feel.

And it is beautiful
how the war inside us
is the only thing that is meant
to make us feel safe,
against a world that has been
designed
to rip us apart
from the moment
we are born.

I Know No End

I was born
into the world,
in all its
bitter gentleness.

I wake up
beneath the cold
and it is
heavy but I can
still breathe.

The show must
go on,
I must go on
and I will never
end
like the love
it has given me.

It Is Not The End

The closer I got to
people, the more alone
I felt.
And their faces would
say more about me
than I could ever of
myself.

Maybe that is why I
felt so empty sometimes.
I left my pieces in
the places that filled
me.

And in the end,
I lost myself
in everything I
knew I loved.

Never Become

We will never be happy,
because our expectation of happiness
is always evolving.
And as we evolve everything changes.
Even the love we have now
becomes something of yesterday
and the anticipation of the things
we desire tomorrow
are the things that fill our emptiness
today.

And as we evolve;
nothing stays the same.
We will always want more
even if what we have now is enough.

This is the destruction of being
human.
We create the illusion of
happiness to make sense of the
disappointments we have yet
to live.

And sometimes we do find happiness,
but even so,
sometimes it is not meant
to last forever
and that within itself
is a beautiful thing to evolve from.

Build & Destroy

Find someone
who is worth
taking you away
from the reality
you have built.

And become someone
who will
inspire others
to design
a reality
worth building.

Walking Blind

We are
too fast
to judge the
faults
in others,
but
too slow
to judge the
faults
within ourselves.

Sometimes
I feel like
I am walking
backwards,
and running in
circles
over
and over
again.

Maybe It Is True

Maybe
we feel
empty
because we
leave
pieces of
ourselves
in all the
things
we used to
love.

Violent Storms

She brought out the storm
in people
because she knew
wherever there were
dark skies and wild winds
slept a truth.
A truth that described
how much love one can leave
behind
the moment they accept
all the pain
they have lived.

And that is all
she ever wanted,
for everyone around her
to embrace their storms
and make love
to their own
violent winds.

Tragic Love

How else did I think this
was going to end?
Yes, it did hurt;
it always does.
I was just that kind of person.
The kind of person who would
always believe in the best
of people and I believed in her
as I watched her kill me slowly.

And I did welcome the pain;
there was no other way to live.
She made me know what it was
like to feel and that was
important to me.

And as the time passed
I still thought about her,
and maybe
one day I would be able to
find her,
and thank her for the tragedy
because it was exactly
what I needed
to set myself apart.

Lost Places

Some people are
lost in their heads.
Some people are
lost in their hearts.
And some people are
so lost
they find the most
beautiful places,
that some of us
will never
live to fill.

I Will Change You

If ever,
you find yourself
lost in me,
tell me
what you see
beneath it all.

And if it is beauty
you seek in madness,
then I welcome
you to stay.

But I can only
promise you this:
after tonight
you will never,
never be the
same.

Not A Tomb

This world is not a tomb for our love.
This world is a door
and it is the door into which our bodies
collide
and where our souls become tidal waves
that do not destroy as they expand,
but rather they collect our memories
as they recede.

This world is not a tomb for our love.
This world is just the beginning
and when our bodies detach themselves
from this place
you and I will find each other
and our story will not end.
We will not end and in the next life
we will stir one another until
the oceans in me
reflect the skies in you.

This world is not a tomb for our love
and though we both know that this
world will end,
it will not be our tomb.

Machines That Kill

How distant
have we all
truly become,
to believe
that the only things
that make us feel
like we are a part
of each others' lives,
are the machines
we created
that drift us all
further apart.

Rain Song

And there were
always
those nights where
she preferred the
rain over people.
Because the rain would
remind her of how
she should feel
and people
would remind her
of all the things
she always
wanted
to forget.

Crash & Burn

I admit
she had a little
madness,
but I didn't care.
She was magic and I
was on the edge.
She wanted to fall and
I wanted to fly.
And somewhere in between
we lost direction
in our heads.

We collided
and I lost my heart
on impact.

Forever Falling

Fall deeply into something
indefinable.
Believe me,
it is a beautiful thing.
Let it grow inside you
until it becomes you
and then let it grow
some more.

And when the indefinable
becomes the familiar,
then I urge you
to keep going,
to keep finding,
there will always be more.
That is your role in life;
to keep on experiencing yourself
until you know so much
that it terrifies you.

Like The Moon

She could not
make sense of the
things
that were meant for her,
but she was drawn
to it all.
And when she was alone,
she felt like
the moon:
terrified of the sky,
but completely
in love
with the way
it held the stars.

Save Us

I can't tell you
exactly how it will end,
but I can say this:
when it begins,
it will feel like the
rain
and when it ends,
it will feel like the
fire.

And the truth is,
we are both
beautifully mad
enough to believe,
that maybe love
was meant to save
us
from ourselves.

Promise

Love me like
there is something
in the air
and it is killing
us softly.

Love me forever,
love me slowly,
love me till you die
and if we ever
lose our way,
promise me
that you will
find me
in all the moments
where I took
your breath
away.

Promise me.

It Does Not Feel The Same

I feel certain
that I will not return
to the world,
that the love
that flows within me
will never stop consuming me,
for it has taken me away
from it all.

And that is exactly what happens
to us
when we fall in love.
We disregard the world
and everyone in it
and believe that nothing
really matters beyond this point,
but the truth is this:
sometimes
we cheat ourselves
from understanding
that when we return,
the world might look the same
but it will not feel
the same way
at all.

Through The Air

We burned through the air
and we convinced
the fire
that we, too, were worthy
of lighting any room
and dimming slowly and softly.

And together
like the sun we rose
and manifested brightly,
and together
like the sunset
we faded off magnificently.
And for that moment in time
I knew what we had
was meant to be
unforgettably beautiful.

And that was just with our eyes;
imagine what it would be like
if ever,
we said hello.

A Dangerous Shore

Maybe it wasn't her.
Maybe it was just
everyone else,
and maybe that's why
we couldn't
understand her.

Maybe she was an
ocean and maybe she
just always made us all
feel
like we were lost
at sea.

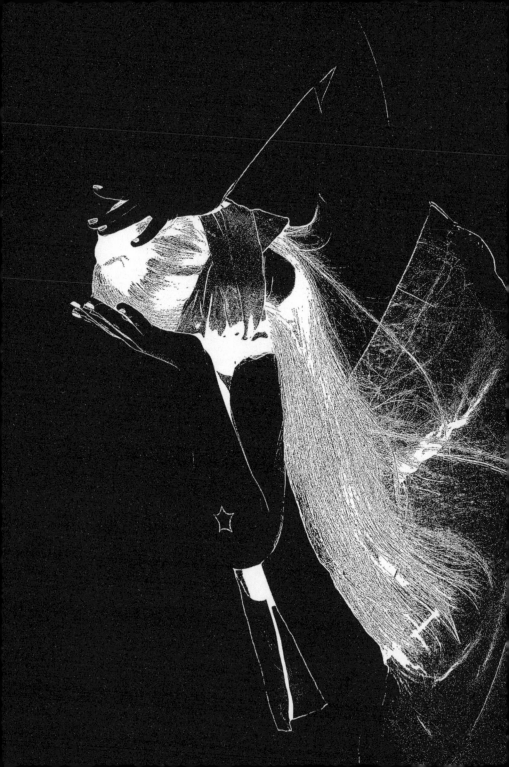

Bright Moons

There was a flower
in her heart;
it just needed more
room to bloom.
And when she set it
free,
she showed the
world
that sometimes
the most beautiful things
can grow in the darkest
of places
without the need
of light.

Letting Go

The hard part is
pretending
not to give a fuck
when you really do.

The worst part is
trying
to close your heart
when its doors
have been blown
to pieces.

Imagine

There is something far greater
than death
and that is to be ignored.
Sometimes I think of all the faces
I have come across
and all the faces
I have forgotten and how terrible
it is to come and go.

Imagine
you meet someone,
and completely forget they exist
the next day.
In a way,
this is how we all live our lives.
We tend to only care about
the moments that make us
feel something;
until we completely devour
the life out of them
and move on to the next
moment that might make us feel
like we are all worth
a little more
than that of the night before.

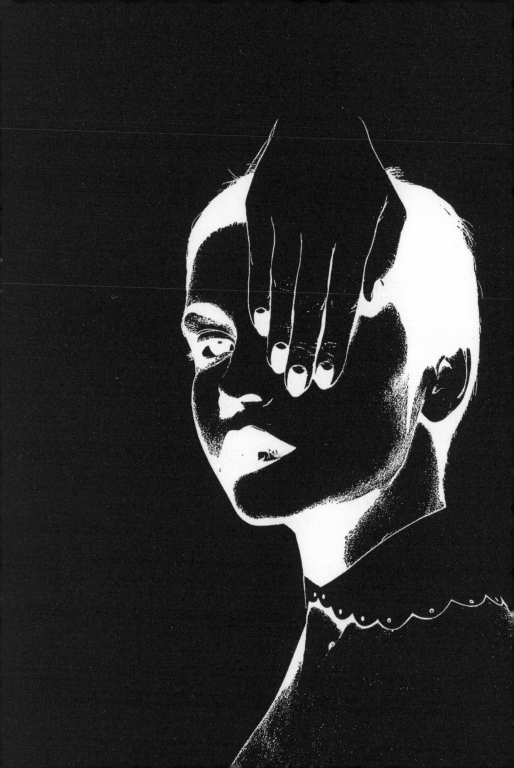

Unwilling

And when I told you
I felt disconnected
from it all,
it really meant
I needed you to
save me.

Save me from all
the things
we were both
unwilling to
let go.

Drowning In You

Maybe I am
a little crazy.

Crazy enough to
love madly
and crazy enough
to love
like pain
was never meant
to reach
the shore.

Changing Tides

There is nothing
more dangerous
to any form of government
than an entire
generation
who knows how to dream
and believe
in themselves enough
to change
and reinvent
it all.

It Does Not Hurt

Maybe it is just the way we are
when we are with each other.
We cannot get it together
or
agree on anything.
And maybe that is what
attracts us;
the fact that you and I
know what is best for one another,
but we are just too afraid
to accept it.
Either way, I am not sure
if I can ever let go
because deep down inside of me
everything begins to hurt
the moment I feel
like looking away.

I Do Believe

Do not wait until
tomorrow,
tomorrow is not
real.
There is only now
and right now
I need you to
believe in yourself
more
than I believe
in you.

Kiss & Kill

Loving me will
not be easy.

It will be war.

You will hold
the gun
and I will hand
you the bullets.

So breathe,
and embrace the
beauty of the
massacre
that lies ahead.

Underwater

You are
not
who you are
when you are
above the water.

You are
who you are
when you return back
to the ocean
and you remember
what it felt like
when you saw
the sky.

Things Change

I know I have not
been the same
and I know there are times
when I look at you
and I feel like
I am staring at someone
I barely know anymore.
And what kills me the most is
that I know
deep down inside,
when you look at me,
you are probably feeling
the same thing.
And there is no other way
to define this
than me losing myself here
and you
finding yourself
somewhere else.

I See You

The truth is,
she did not
need to be saved;
she just needed
to feel loved
and know
that someone
out there
craved her
attention.

Feel The Moment

Sometimes
we just need someone.
It does not matter
who it is.
Just someone,
someone to remind us
of what it is like
to live in a moment
and feel
something
before we walk away.

War On My Skin

How violently
beautiful
would it be to leave
your mind here
and
your body somewhere else.

This is the way
you make me feel
when your fingertips
declare war on my
skin.

Born To Fly

You have thought about what
the world thinks for so long
that you could hardly recognize
yourself anymore.

Imagine, being born to fly
but being placed in a cage
where you could barely stretch
out your own wings.

You could still be
so many things and there is
so much more of you to be found.

So fly,
fly away and never return
to a world that makes
you feel like you are trapped,
and you do not know
who you are.

The Chaos In Me

The worst thing
you could do is
tame the chaos in you.
It is like
being told not to feel
when you are
walking through
the fire.

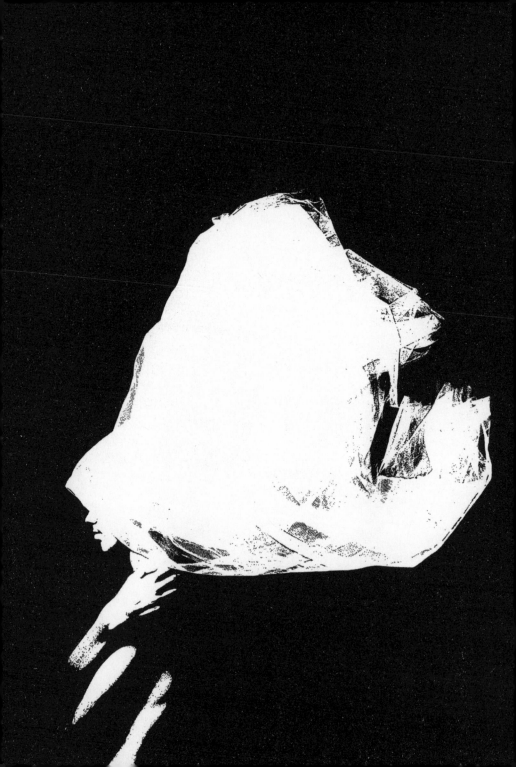

Find Your Path

Don't think.
It complicates things.
Just feel, and
if it feels like home
then follow
its path.

Strange Fiction

Perhaps,
in some sense,
what we consider reality
is in fact
the strangest piece of fiction
we will all
ever
live to know.

It Never Ends

I began to have symptoms of you.
I began to think and talk like you.
I laughed like you,
I walked like you,
and I even began to smile like you.
I missed you so much that
I became you.

And as the year passed,
I heard rumors that you became me too.
And when we finally crossed,
we stood silently in front of each other
and I felt like I fell off the edge
of the earth.

I knew what we had was not over,
we were not done
and we did not know how to make
our love end.

The Waves Know

And the ocean taught
her how to drown
in all the things
bigger than herself.
The ocean loved her
and knew everything
that made her
and every time
she would walk to
the shore,
she would smile at
the ocean
because the waves
knew her story.

Horrors Of The Heart

She was never crazy.
She just didn't let
her heart settle
in a cage.
She was born wild
and sometimes we
need people like her.
For it's the horrors
in her heart
which cause the flames
in ours.

And she was always
willing to burn
for everything she
has ever loved.

Who We Are

We spend our lives
looking for reasons
to stay
but sometimes leaving
is the only
thing we are meant
to share.

So why try to be
anything
more than we are meant
to become.

Maybe coming and going
is what makes us
who we are.

Fallen Deeply

And every time
I look at you,
I can feel something
stirring inside of me.
Like a collection
of dying stars
drowning beneath the waves.

Waves that belong
to your ocean
and I have fallen deeply
without really knowing
how far
it all could go.

Dark Dreams

I'm not who I was
yesterday and maybe
you're still the same
person in my memories.
I can't tell the
difference between what
was and what is.
I just know beneath
everything you left
behind, I found a dark
paradise, where you
and I were forever
and you and I were one.

Salvation In Art

I would like to be
the necessary
and not the obvious.
I would like to be
the only thing
that could exist
in your sentence.

I want to be more
than just words.

I want to be
your art,
I want to be
your salvation.

Art is the only
thing that allows
us to be ourselves.

Edge Of The World

I have let
too many nights
pass
without telling you
how your love
is so beautiful and full.
And how it blooms
in the darkness
and how it is
the only thing
I can see;
distantly burning
like a candle
on the edge of the world.

Connects Inside

If you ever
forget who you are,
always remember
that you are everything
you know you are not.

And if you cannot remember
that,
then remember this:
you are every moment
that is meant
to be remembered.
You are everything
that matters
and you are everything
that makes sense
to all the little things
that connect inside
of you.

Alone By The Sun

Just to think
we share the same
sky and breathe
the same air.
Perhaps, that is
all I will ever
need.

To know that maybe
someone out there
was meant for me.

So I would not
feel too alone.

Beautiful Horrors

Leave your horrors
with me, they are
beautiful.
Leave all the things
you have always
wanted to forget
and leave everything
else that hurts.
I will show you
that you are not
crazy.
You are just a little
different
and I have always
been a sucker
for that.

Types Of Feelings

You begin to feel
like you are not yourself lately.
You begin to laugh
and you begin to smile
a little more often.
And for a second time
you begin to discover
yourself again.

This is the kind of feeling
people have
when they start to believe
in something bigger
than themselves.
And this is the kind of feeling
I get when I am lost;
submerged
somewhere deep
inside of your soul.

Be Destroyed

There must be
about a million ways to let
yourself
be destroyed,
but then there is you
and I think tonight
I am in the mood
to break apart
and let myself be consumed
by all
the things
I know
I would never be able
to recover from.

Burning Scar

And in the end,
she left a scar
and I knew that was
how she wanted to
be remembered.

She wanted to leave
her mark in the
world
without getting
her heart too
attached to it.

Robin Williams

I could never take
myself too seriously.
I wanted the whole
world to smile
with me,
and I wanted to fill
their empty spaces
with laughter.

So when I departed
from their eyes,
their hearts would
remember how
beautiful it is
to feel.

Wild Wind

If only
we knew how to stop
waiting for all
the things
that are not meant
to arrive;
then perhaps,
some of us
would finally let go
and learn how to fly
against
the wild wind.

Rioting Bloom

She did not find
the grim
in falling apart,
for every time
she found herself
to be broken,
she knew
that she was brutally
remaking herself
and collapsing
to be reborn
like a rioting star;
haunting
the dark sky.

The Things I Can Lose

Without a little madness
I wouldn't be able
to feel.
And if I can't feel
then I'll lose my mind.
And if I lose my mind
then I'll lose my words.

This is how I love,
madly enough to lose
myself and feel all the
things I can't
put into words.

Please Stay

The beauty of not
knowing how you feel
is that
one day you will realize
that not knowing
was the only way
you would find all
the feelings
that were meant
to stay.

Things Do Come Back

I know when we go we come back
as the things we admired most.
So when I told you I admired
autumn and you told me you admired
the way children laugh,
that stuck on me.
And in the end, I know
some of us will come back as the rain,
while others will come back as flowers.

So if I come back
as a falling leaf stumbling toward
the ground,
just promise me you will come back
in the imagination of a child
and you will inspire me to become
something more
than what I really am.

Beautiful Words

You are going to come across
people in your life
who will inspire you,
love you and change you.

And that is a rare thing.

But every once in a while
you will come across
someone
who will completely rob you
from your sleep,
and those are the people
who are just
too beautiful to put
into words.

No Sleep

Dreams
were always drawn
to call her name
and
reality just
could not
learn to let
her go.

Nothing Is Left

Some people are meant
to stay
while others are meant
to leave.
And there is really
no difference between
the two
except the way you change
after you realize
you have nothing else
left to give.

Curious Feel

We are here,
but before we forget
why we came,
let us remember well,
that this
is the way we all
tend to begin;
with a little curiosity
for something
that is meant
to make us feel real.

Dark Seconds

Do not detach your face
and point it toward
the stars,
you will not
find yourself in the heavens.
You will find yourself
when you stand in the center
and explode
to light up the dark
for a few seconds.

In our last moments
we will be defined
by how we lit the clouds
and time will pass
and we will be forgotten
but the sky
will remember our names.

Never Sorry

She was never sorry for
not knowing how to end
and not knowing how to
be a memory.
She was never sorry for
not letting the world
turn her cold.

And most of all, she
was never sorry for
learning how to love
so deeply
and for moving these
people around her
in ways their bodies
could never imagine.

Do Not Wait

When I look at you
I can't remember
what I'm waiting for.
I forget who I am and
I forget why I even
came.

This is how I want to
live; like I'm lost
in something I love
and every moment I
spend is like I'm
waiting,
waiting for something
inspiring to
happen.

Love Meant

She was so many things and I never
understood why she always wanted
to be so different.
I tried to define her every time
she changed because I, too,
would change and then it all just
changed.

Or maybe she was never
here and I was always waiting,
waiting for a girl with too much
inside her.

A girl with the kind
of story that would ache my soul,
because I knew it was not meant to
last, but also because I knew that
this was the only way love was
meant to go.

Accidents Happen

People come and go;
they take something
and leave
but the relationship between
you and other people
is easy.

Just keep the ones
who want that little light
inside of you,
that little light
you cannot even explain yourself.
Everyone else
is just a coincidence;
a little accident
waiting to happen.

Sad Soul

Maybe one day
we will find that
place
where you and I could
be together.
And we will catch
our dreams within the
waves of change.

So smile for me one
last time and believe
that we will meet
again.

Until then,
I will be missing you.

A Lover's Smile

The most
dangerous
lover
is one
who greets
the pain
with a smile.

Night Beast

And every once in a while
it would just hit me;
the horrifying truth
of being alone.

And it did not matter
if I was with good or bad company.
I would slowly feel
the violent pull of loneliness,
shaking
inside of me
like a wild beast
in the night.

Terrible Darkness

And when I looked back at my life,
when I looked back at it all,
I clearly saw how bad times
really meant everything.
And how every moment
that led me to happiness,
revolved around some kind
of terrible darkness.

Sometimes the darkness
was a beautiful thing
and sometimes it took me to a place
where I had no idea
where it all could go,
but I knew it was all meant
to be okay.

Directions To My Heart

My mind will depart now
and the next time it is
here, it will not
be the same.

So good-bye little thoughts,
fly away,
and take my fears with you.

And if ever you return
then give direction to
my heart,
so it can never stop
believing in all the
things I will never
live to understand.

Leave My Love Behind

I just want to tell everyone
what I was like.
I want you all to know
how much I felt.
I want you all to tell them
how my story was not hard
but how it was inspiring.

Tell them I existed.
Tell them how much I lived.

And above all, tell them
all how much I loved.

Lovely Madness

You look at lovers,
the way they are with each other
and it makes you sick,
for how could two people
be in love
and then the next day
be complete strangers.

And when you think about love,
you feel that it must be something
only crazy people do . . .
until it finds you, because it will.
And when it does it will grab you
and shake the madness
out of you.
Only to discover that,
that little touch of crazy
has always been inside you too.

Love is beautiful
but love too can
be terrible.

Good-bye Tonight

We will not be
the same after tonight
and knowing this
we still smile
and say good-bye.

This is
how it operates;
this is
how change happens.

The Last Request

I'm sorry I can't
save the world;
I don't want any part
in that.
I just want to be
remembered in a way
where I can mean
everything
to one person
and save them,
save them from all
the insecurities
this world has created.

Bury Me Now

The simple truth
how sometimes we are
not meant to be restored,
how we are not meant
to feel at home,
and how we are not meant
to live easy.

Sometimes our thoughts
rage like wild fires
and our bodies stay perfectly
still.

The world wants to kill
us, but we are all already dead.
Death will come easy
and everything else is
too hard.

Something we will never
be able to understand.

Similarities

Some things never change;
like that feeling you get
when you haven't seen someone
for some time now.
That feeling of two people
starting right where they left off.

And then, some things do change
like two people growing further apart,
but also remembering
the little things,
the little similarities that string
them back together,
as if nothing ever happened
or
as if nothing ever drifted them
apart.

Differences

When we have something
we want more
and when we have nothing
we want something.

We always tend to want
the things we can't have
and in a strange way . . .

that makes us all the same.

Pretending To Live

They're not like
you and I,
they just don't get it.
They don't see
chaos as beauty
or
self-destruction as birth.
They don't know what
to feel and they don't
know how to be themselves.

But most of all,
they just don't know how
to live.

Sensing It All

I just want you to help me
finish my story.
I want it to end with
confusion, and I never
want to make sense of all
the things this world
has made me feel.

Because we should never
give reason for being.

For being is all we know
when everything else
just doesn't seem to
make any sense at all.

Moving On

The older you get
the more people disappear
and that's how it works.
One day you are missing the company
of someone
and then the next day
you remember a little less
that they are gone.
You adapt to the change
and it doesn't make you
a bad person to move on;

that's life
and that's just how people are.

Where We Belong

We belong to other people.
We belong in their photographs,
in their memories,
and in their hearts,
because sometimes that is all we have.
The idea of wanting
to belong to someone,
to someone who tells us that they
need us just as much as we need
them and that is what the
meaning of life should be.
To feel loved and to give it
back and nothing else, because
honestly everything else does not
matter, everything else is just a map
and that map might lead us to a hole
filled with quiet deserts
and empty spaces.

Art Is Pain

Art is pain
and
pain is the
art
in which
we find
ourselves.

I'm Sorry I Left

I understand you just
wanted someone to reach
you,
when you felt like you
had been gone
for some time now.

Maybe I failed you
and maybe things could
have been different.

If only I had known,
then perhaps,
when I returned,
you would have stayed
the same.

Run Closer

There are some days
where I feel
like no matter where I go,
I always end up feeling the same,
because
all places are the same
in the end.

Or maybe it's just me
and no matter where I go,
I could never
run far enough from who I am,
and I could never run far enough
from everything
that hurts.

Young At Heart

She had such a beautiful mind.
The kind of mind
that sparked my dreams,
the kind of mind
that led my inspiration
and it was the kind of inspiration
that only
the young at heart
could imagine.

Old Friend

I can tell you're
not yourself
lately and I hope
wherever you've
gone, you feel free.

Calm Your Storms

I see all these people
but I can't see their faces.
I've been to all these cities
and I can't remember what
they look like.

I feel things, things that
make me ignore the things I
should be doing.

So yes, I've gone mad
but let me say this:
my heart is the best part of
me and it will always calm
the storm for all of those
who are afraid of a little rain.

Healing Drugs

We say
time will heal everything,
but time will never
be on our side.

For time has only
taught us regret
and
regret has always
been a terrible drug.

Empty Rooms

There are some things
that are meant to vanish
in an instant
and then there are some things
that will take time
to dissolve.

And it is the same way
with people.
Some of them will disappear
into the air,
while others will slowly burn
out of our lives.

Life has a funny way
of making us feel less alone
because in the end,
all that remains
are empty rooms.

I Do Not Fall Easy

I can't remember what it
was like before you,
and I don't even know how
we got here
but maybe that's exactly
what I needed.

Someone who could make
me forget where I came from
and someone who could
make me love
without knowing how to fall.

At all.

Understanding Me

I can feel you through
your lonely eyes
and I hope one day you'll
understand
how everything that
hurt us
was everything that
made us who we are.

Unlocked Cages

I found hell in my head
and heaven in other people;
they could never collide
at the same time.
And when they did
I was still burning
in the fire.

Sometimes I feel like my life
is a wild beast
trapped in an unlocked cage
and it is awfully
afraid of what lies
on the other side.

That is what hell is like;
having something
viciously brilliant inside of you,
but not believing in it enough
to set it free.

Live Die Less

Life has been too repetitive.
We are more like machines
than we are people.
We forget how to
feel,
appreciate,
and love.

We are caught up by the temporary;
distracted by nothing.
There is no war among us,
but the war within ourselves.
People fear breaking the rules.
Go out there;
the air is waiting for you.

Learn to live a little.
Learn to die a lot less.

It Must Be Real

Sometimes
you change the way I feel,
and sometimes
the way I feel is the
darkest place
and sometimes
the darkest place is the
only place
where we could discover
something real.

Tonight It Is Us

All we have is
each other
but we carry our
insecurities like we
are not sure where
we belong.

So do not look back,
come as you are
and I promise you;
after tonight,
everything will be
beautiful.

Freedom Sense

People hurt people
and that's how it works.
If we didn't hurt each other
could you imagine how awfully perfect
the world would be?
It would be a horrible place.

Sometimes the pain is the only thing
that makes sense to the soul
and sometimes
it's the only thing we need
to experience
the beautiful freedom
we all deserve.

Slipping Air

Maybe there was
something out there,
something
that understood you
and for some odd reason
you let it slip away.

That's life
and sometimes
that's love.

I Never Left You

I hope one day
you will realize
how you were
never alone.
Because you were
here once
and I have always been
with you
even when you were out
searching for
yourself.

Scary Movies

Love will never be easy
and knowing so
we accept the horrors
that some types of love
are meant to kill us
one way or another.
Too much or too little of it
can only mean
we are looking for some kind
of trouble.

Sometimes love
is that fucked up movie
where everyone dies
in the end.

Broken Hours

Here is one simple fact
I have learned about people.
No one ever stays the same.
Some come, some go,
and some never return.
Some take, some give,
and some only dream.
Some want to be, while others
just are.
Some begin, some end,
and some just never start at all.
Some are bright, some are dim,
and some are always wishing
they were more.

It never ends.

People are like hours;
they are changing
all the time.

She Eats Thunder

She was thunder and her
smile would rattle my bones.
She couldn't pile herself
together but I fell in love,
I fell in love with all of
her.

She was the death of me,
the beginning and the end.
And I never understood her,
for how could someone
so beautiful be the cause
of so much destruction
after all.

Ghostly Memories

There is something beautiful
about the past
and about the way it haunts us.
The way we pass through moments
like walking through doors.
The way we shut some out
and the way we welcome some
to stay.

Our memories are ghosts,
and they will always
remind us
of all the things we
no longer have.

Endless Repeat

It's terrible the way we hurt
each other unconsciously,
but I don't know what's worse,
the fact that we hurt certain people
in our lives
without knowing or the fact
that we keep on hurting
the same people,
the very same way.

Sometimes
our lives are made up
of the same stories with the same
beginnings
and the same endings
and things happen the same way
almost every time.

Truth Hurts

My love is not a product
of the world,
but a product of all
the people I have met.

And through everyone
I have ever come across,
I discovered that
our disconnect was
never because of the
insecurities we felt,
but rather
the emptiness we created
when we failed to
make sense of ourselves.

Bloom Again

There is nothing here again,
but there is so much to find.
For sometimes
I feel like I have lost it all:
mind and soul.
And it is only getting harder
to tell the difference
between what I love and what I do not
when the only flower
in my heart is wanting
to bloom again.

Reborn

Some people try so hard
to change
but sometimes it doesn't happen that way;
we cannot force it,
it takes time.
Sometimes it just happens overnight,
like one day it all makes sense
and just like that
you change.

That should be inspiring to us all,
the way we are able to die every night;
only to be reborn the next day
for the rest of our lives.

Defeat Is Love

My Dear,
My life has been well-lived
on the edge,
but when I fell
it felt like I was falling
for a thousand years.
And when I got up
I felt young again,
I felt alive
and what a beautiful thing it was;
to feel defeated.

Where I no longer had to fight,
the war was over
and all that was left to do
was love.

When Words Fail

There are ways
of understanding people
that do not require words,
and if you look close enough
you will see,
a lot of life
and a little bit of death
burning through their eyes.
And sometimes
that says more
than we could ever explain
or
imagine about ourselves.

Change You, Change Us

I want to change people.
I want them to learn how to
feel each other.
How to lose and find themselves
in the eyes of a stranger.

I want them all to feel like
they are not alone,
that we are all in this
together
and I hope that never
changes.

Imagine that, what a
beautiful way to live,
what a beautiful way to feel,
and what a beautiful
way to survive.

Things Strike Me

There is nothing out here . . .
it is all inside;
it is all in my head.
The things that happen do not exist
unless I give them meaning.
To be able to define everything
is where my greatest weakness lies.
To be able to feel
is the madness I need to make sense
of the things that strike me.
People strike me,
love strikes me,
and everything else moves me
in such a way
that I could barely understand.
I feel,
and everything I feel is nothing;
nothing but an extension
of the mind
and
of the heart I was born with.

Stolen Magic

I have been taking as much as
I can
from other people:
the way they spoke,
their words would fill me.
Their look,
their story,
and the way they said good-bye.
I took so much that I was no longer here,
but rather I was lost
in all of them
and I knew that I would never
be able to find myself again.

You see I felt so empty;
that I was collecting people
like souvenirs
and I was filling myself with the magic
I knew others had to offer.

Made Myself

I made myself
from all the photographs
I never took,
from all the love
I never received,
and
from all the moments
that never happened.

And it has been too real,
it has been
a beautiful struggle;
one that has always
reminded me
of how easy
it was to laugh.

Dear Charise,
May your flame live within
my heart and continue
to inspire me through
every waking hour.

With open eyes I see the world,
with an open heart I see the souls,
and with an open mind I see it all differently.

Thank you for your time.

Robert M. Drake

In Memory of
Guillermo Rodriguez
06/25/1985 - 08/25/2014

The last time we spoke you told me you were proud
of me, and that I was your brother since day one.
Well . . . this is me telling you that you're my brother
and I miss you. See you soon.

I wrote all of these words for you.

CHASING THE GLOOM

COMING SOON

SUNFLOWER

ROBERT M. DRAKE

A NOVELLA
COMING SOON...

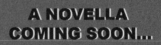

Also Available

ROBERT M. DRAKE
SPACESHIP

Also Available

ROBERT M. DRAKE

SCIENCE

Also Available

ROBERT M. DRAKE

Beautiful
Chaos

Follow R. M. Drake
for excerpts and updates.

Facebook.com/rmdrk
Twitter.com/rmdrk
Instagram.com/rmdrk
rmdrk.tumblr.com